boo-hoo!

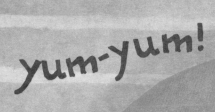

# BABY FACES

A Book
of Happy,
Silly, Funny
Babies

KATE
MERRITT

hurray!

kiss!

wow!

night-night!

# BOOKS BABIES CAN REALLY SINK THEIR GUMS INTO!

Are you feeling happy? Hurray!
Are you feeling sad? Boo-hoo!
Are you feeling hungry? Yum-yum!

Share baby's many moods in a book that's INDESTRUCTIBLE

*Dear Parents:* INDESTRUCTIBLES are built for the way babies "read": with their hands and mouths. INDESTRUCTIBLES won't rip or tear and are 100% washable. They're made for baby to hold, grab, chew, pull, and bend.

Chew them all!

WORKMAN PUBLISHING
225 Varick Street
York, NY 10014
workman.com

$8.95
IN/AU CANADA

THOMAS ALLEN & SON SINCE 1916

978-0-7611-6881-2

50595
9 780761 168812